Collectible

Costume Jewelry

Revised Edition

S. Sylvia Henzel

On the Cover, clockwise l to r: Pink powder box, satin finish glass, C. 1920, **$65.** Tiny Art Nouveau jewelry box, thin gold plate over base metal, **$25.** Large Victorian silver-plated jewelry box with purple velvet lining, **$125.** Hand-cut quartz or clear rock crystal faceted beads, knotted, 22″ length, **$325.** Wristwatch, gold case, 15 jewels, two adjustments, in running condition, **$150.** Attached to watchband, gold locket with tiny diamond, **$110.** Gold bracelet with flower design on front, **$175.** Ring with genuine amethyst in a 14k gold filigree basket setting, **$275.** Gold ring, 22k, with initial "S", **$175.**

Photographs: Tom Gregorka
Cover Design: Ann Eastburn
Interior Layout: Anthony Jacobson

Library of Congress Catalog
Card Number 87-50013

ISBN 0-87069-496-0

10   9   8   7   6   5   4   3

Published by

A Capital Cities/ABC, Inc. Company

Wallace-Homestead Book Company
201 King of Prussia Road
Radnor, Pennsylvania 19089

Introduction

Since my first book, *Old Costume Jewelry: A Collector's Dream,* was published in 1978, much of the once available old costume jewelry has found its way into collections. Many fine pieces then available are now scarce. However, opportunities still remain for the knowledgeable collector to find desirable, collectible items. This book will aid the novice and average collector in identifying and pricing many of those pieces. The jewelry pictured in this book can still be found, although demand has reduced the availability of some of the items.

The prices shown are a compilation of those seen in antique shops, antique shows, and flea markets, combined with firsthand experience buying and selling old costume jewelry for many years. Scarcity and demand, type of material, and artistic design are factors that determine value. The prices given are for jewelry in perfect condition.

A careful and discerning collector can still, with some patience, acquire an enviable collection of old costume jewelry. The collector's rewards are derived from participation in an exciting and fascinating field of collecting and from the enjoyment of owning pieces that are almost certain to appreciate in value. Such pleasures account for the continuing popularity that collecting old costume jewelry enjoys.

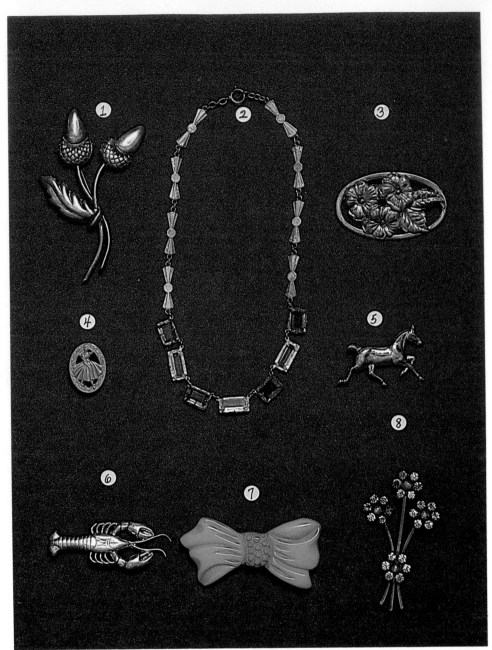

(1) Twin acorn brooch, heavyweight sterling silver marked "A.H. Texco 940" pure, **$65.** (2) Art Deco necklace, polished base metal with imitation amethyst and clear stones, **$75.** (3) Brooch, sterling silver moss roses in oval frame, **$45.** (4) Gold-plated brooch, Style Makers award pin, **$25.** (5) Brooch, sterling silver, running horse, **$35.** (6) Brooch, lobster, sterling silver, applied hallmark by Lang, **$45.** (7) Brooch, plastic bow, Art Nouveau, **$45.** (8) Brooch, base metal, imitation stones, **$18.**

(1) Wooden beads, C.1920, **$28.** (2) Ruby colored, pressed glass beads, 15½″ long, Art Deco, **$65.** (3) Blue paste beads, C.1920, **$45.** (4) Bar pin brooch, enamel on brass, **$28.** (5) Brooch, ivory carved roses on enameled branch, **$75.**

(1) Drop earrings, screw posts, overlay, possibly Czechoslovakian, **$18.** (2) Celluloid bracelet, machine-stamped, high relief, **$45.** (3) Celluloid brooch, coral colored, **$45.** (4) Celluloid bracelet, amber color with matching paste stones, **$55.** (5) Bracelet, gold wash over base metal, **$45.** (6) Celluloid bracelet with paste stones, **$45.** (7) Brooch, gold wash over base metal, **$15.** (8) Art Nouveau earrings, water lilies, sterling, **$65.** (9) Earrings, turtles, with paste stones, screw posts, **$22.** (10) American Indian design sterling bracelet, **$55.** (11) Plastic cameo earrings on gold-washed base metal, screw posts, **$45.** (12) Heavy sterling silver earrings, screw posts, **$35.** (13) Cuff-type bracelet, gold wash over base metal, **$45.** (14) Art Deco plastic brooch, **$35.**

(1) Beads made from horn dyed to look like amber, **$55.** (2) Plastic cherries brooch, early 1930s, **$35.** (3) Art Deco beads made from horn, **$55.** (4) Horse-shoe-shaped celluloid brooch with beads made to look like amber, **$55.** (5) Brooch, abalone in base metal frame, **$12.** (6) Enamel-on-copper brooch with tiny buckle pin, **$45.** (7) Vanity case, never used, new condition, print under glass, chromium metal, **$55.**

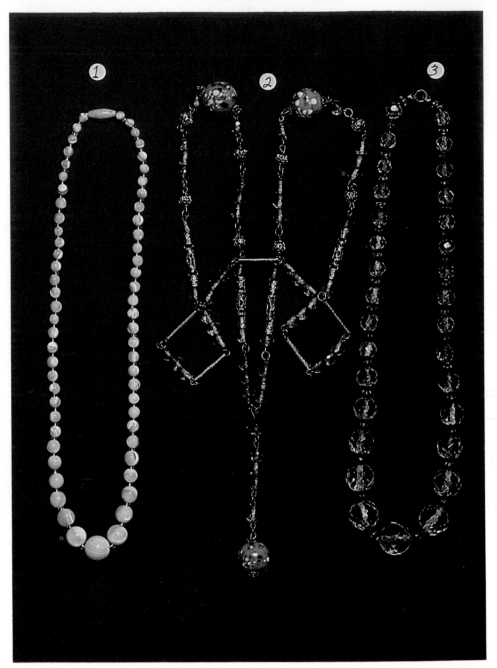

(1) Mother-of-pearl beads have been reproduced. Old ones pictured have a mellow, cream-colored shade. New ones are very white, **$38.** (2) Glass beads interspaced with silver metal findings, 19¾″ long, **$75.** (3) Clear glass faceted beads, each interspaced with two black beads, **$28.**

(1) Rare, black shell pearl necklace. These are nearly flat on a double chain, gold-plated clasp, beautiful iridescence, **$250.** (2) Glass beads on brass chain, silver metal findings, 18½″ long, **$85.** (3) Art Deco brooch, imitation amethysts in a beaded white metal frame, applied hallmark "Lidz Bros. N.Y.," **$75.** (4) Necklace, imitation moss agate heart on a low karat gold chain, **$95.** (5) Vanity case, figures by a lake with swans, **$55.**

Art glass beads with a enameled brass finding fitted to each side of each bead, possibly Russian, **$185.** (2) Antique lavaliere set with a beautiful imitation of real lapis lazuli, brass filigree ornaments and findings, **$350.** (3) Beads, dyed horn to look like real jet, **$45.** (4) Brooch, lacy brass with imitation topaz stones, **$25.**

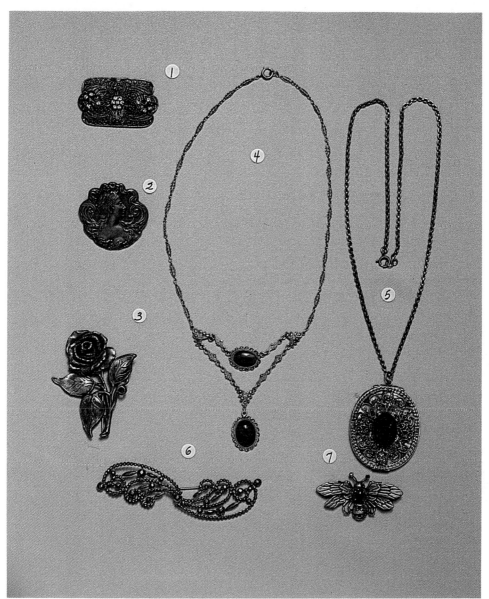

(1) Lacy brass brooch with paste stones, **$28.** (2) Heavyweight sterling silver Art Nouveau brooch, **$350.** (3) Oxidized white metal brooch with beautiful relief work on roses, **$30.** (4) Sterling silver necklace with marcasites and two dark blue paste stones, **$125.** (5) Locket, white base metal characteristic of silver in filigree work, pressed glass cameo, **$32.** (6) Imitation hand-cut steel brooch, stamp-cut by machine, C. 1870-1880, **$65.** (7) Heavyweight sterling silver bee brooch, red paste garnets, **$65.**

(1) Art Deco necklace, low karat gold plated flexible mesh chain, **$40.** (2) These beads resemble angel skin coral, but when tested they proved to be celluloid. Jewelry in celluloid is scarce, **$55.** (3) Plastic brooch looks like ivory, machine stamped, **$18.** (4) Mother-of-pearl brooch in full-back sterling frame, **$18.** (5) Carved ivory brooch, two lilies, **$65.** (6) Bar pin, hand painted brooch in brass frame with six prongs, possible French origin, **$55.** (7) Sterling silver brooch, paste amethyst, **$48.**

(1) Pressed celluloid beads from the early 1920s, **$40.** (2) Celluloid brooch with unusual design. Buttonlike ornaments are hooked on a celluloid chain by small brace rings, **$25.** (3) Scottie dog brooch, C. 1920, gold wash over base metal, black enameled outline, **$20.** (4) Gold wash over brass earrings, green paste stones, screw posts, **$28.** (5) Brooch, base metal with paste stones, **$28.** (6) Art Deco earrings, in sterling silver with paste stones, **$28.** (7) Pressed glass cameo set in sterling silver frame, **$35.** (8) Art Glass period beads. Each bead is actually two beads. The inner beads with goldstone flecks are enclosed in clear glass outer beads. The beads have a brass finding on each side, and every head is different in size. **$250.**

13

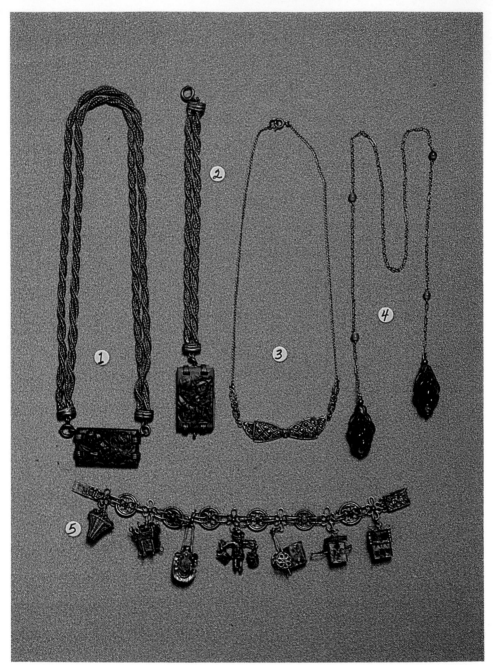

(1) Lavaliere has pressed glass lapis lazuli stone, hooks at side of pendant, gold-washed chain, **$150.** (2) Bracelet matching lavaliere, **$125.** (3) Art Deco necklace, sterling silver with marcasites, **$175.** (4) Art Nouveau loop-over lavaliere, imitation jade with white metal chain, **$85.** (5) Bracelet, with enameled on sterling silver, beautifully detailed charms. Today it would be very expensive to hand enamel these tiny objects, **$350.**

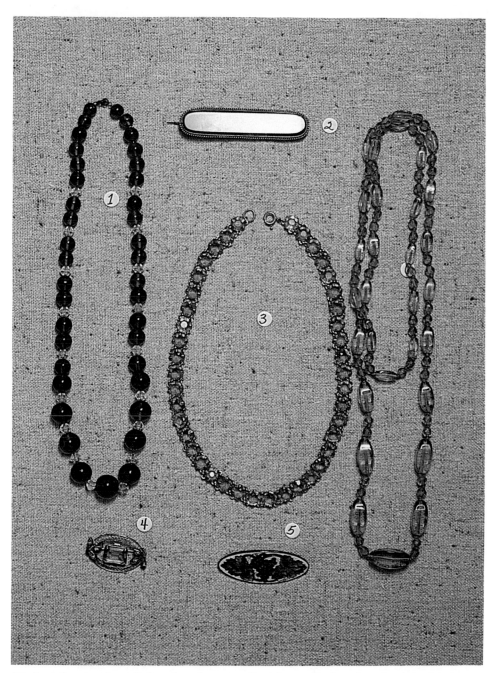

(1) Amethyst colored glass beads spaced with small clear beads, **$55.** (2) Agate bar pin brooch in a beaded brass frame, C.1865, **$95.** (3) Necklace, imitation topaz stones, prong set, flexible, **$35.** (4) Brooch, white base metal characteristic of silver, all glass stones, **$28.** (5) Art Nouveau brooch, cloisonné on copper, **$48.** (6) Blue glass beads, 14″ long, **$45.**

15

(1) Sterling silver brooch with "Lang" applied hallmark, **$40.** (2) Brooch, metal base, all paste stones, **$25.** (3) Glass beads from the Roaring Twenties, **$85.** (4) Brooch, luster enamel on sterling silver, **$85.** (5) Sterling silver brooch with marcasites. The center has a diamond-shaped, pierced design, **$95.** (6) Brooch of red paste garnets and rose glass hearts set in a heart-shaped brass mountings. Hearts are soldered to form a circle, C. 1865, **$125.**

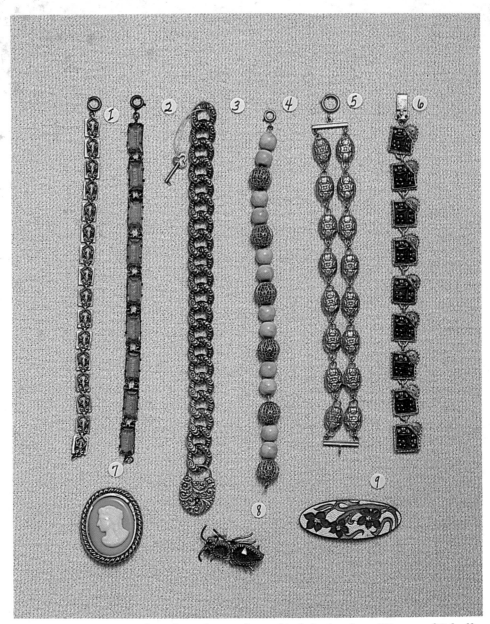

(1) Unusual sterling silver bracelet with applied design has "Danecraft" hall-mark, **$65.** (2) Bracelet with amber paste stones set in pronged, open back mountings of base metal, **$48.** (3) Gold-filled bracelet, expandable with lock and key, **$85.** (4) Bracelet, imitation jade, each bead interspaced with a filigreed brass bead, **$55.** (5) Double strand bracelet, gold-washed, oval-shaped beads on a chain, **$40.** (6) Bracelet, dark blue paste stones ornamented with spun wire, made in Czechoslovakia, **$55.** (7) Pressed glass cameo brooch in a gold-washed frame, **$55.** (8) Brooch, paste amethyst stones set in brass; an early piece, **$55.** (9) Art Nouveau, cloisonné on copper brooch, **$65.**

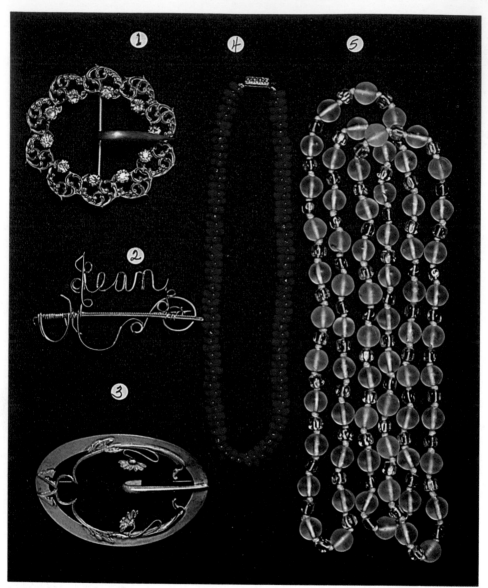

(1) Buckle, gold wash over brass, **$65.** (2) Brooch, gold wire formed, **$85.** (3) Art Nouveau brooch, **$55.** (4) Red coral paste beads, marked "Made in Czechoslovakia," **$45.** (5) Necklace with large, satin-finished beads interspaced with small, topaz-colored beads, 20½" long, **$55.**

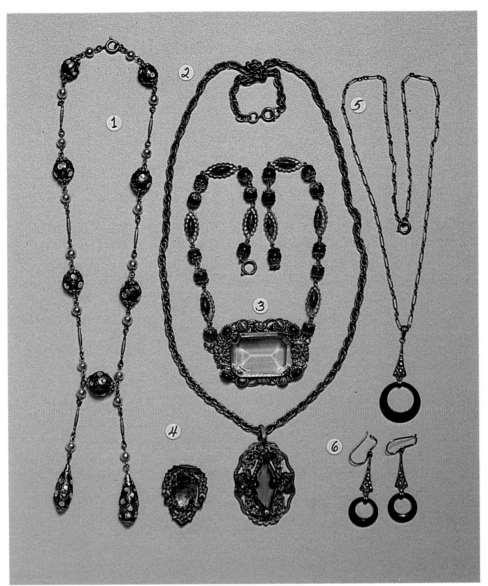

(1) Art Glass period necklace with silver-foil-look beads overlaid with irregular, deep blue glass threads and pale blue dots. No two beads exactly alike. Imitation pearls have white metal findings linked on a silver-type metal chain, **$150.** (2) Lavaliere with a beautiful aquamarine paste stone drop set in a filigree brass frame with six different colored stones, brass chain, **$65.** (3) Lavaliere, paste ornaments on brass chain interspaced with lacy brass findings. Drop has enameled flowers, leaves. Marked "Made in Czechoslovakia," **$55.** (4) Clip, paste topaz stone on a base metal frame with beautiful enameling, **$55.** (5) Art Deco necklace in sterling silver with marcasites and black glass drops, **$85.** (6) Matching earrings, posts have been replaced for wirers, **$75.** *(Jewelry pictured from the collection of Mrs. Joy De Lucco.)*

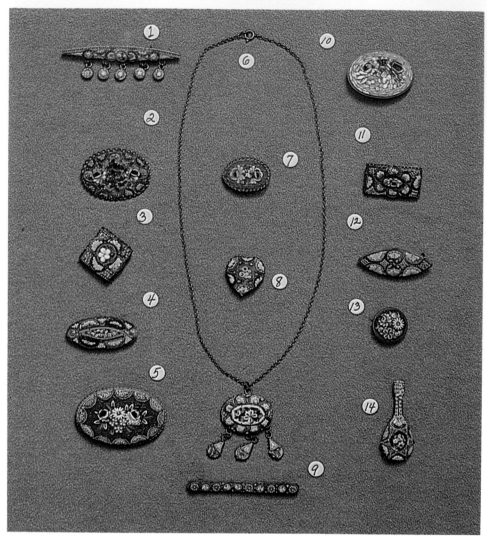

The mosaic jewelry pictured is all C. 1880-1920. (1) Bar pin brooch, brass frame and raised beaded edge, **$95.** (2) Brooch, gray background, very fine work, brass frame with a flat twisted wire edge, **$75.** (3) Square brooch, brass frame with beaded edge, **$45.** (4) Oval brooch, brass frame with beaded edge, **$45.** (5) Oval brooch, red background, brass frame with two types of rope with twisted edge, **$65.** (6) Pendant necklace with three drops in brass frames with beaded edges on rope twist chain of brass, **$125.** (7) Brooch, coral-colored background with applied link chain edge, **$45.** (8) Heart-shaped brooch with beaded edge brass frame, **$50.** (9) Bar pin brooch, very fine detail, has applied rope twist edge, **$85.** (10) Oval brooch, brass frame has beaded edge with applied rope twist, **$45.** (11) Rectangular brooch, brass frame with beaded edge, **$50.** (12) Marquise-style brooch, brass frame with applied rope twist, **$55.** (13) Round brooch, brass frame with applied rope twist edge, **$85.** (14) Brooch, musical instrument, fine detail, **$65.**

(1) Necklace, topaz colored glass beads on a 12½″ chain. Flowerlike findings fitted to each side of the beads, **$45.** (2) Necklace of paste garnets has unusual clasp, **$95.** (3) Beads, red celluloid, 25″ long, **$55.** (4) Earrings, paste stones, screw posts, **$25.** (5) Earrings, amber-colored paste stones on lacy brass, screw posts, **$30.**

(1) Ring, brown sardonyx, gold-plated setting, **$65.** (2) Art Nouveau ring cannot be photographed to its best advantage. It is heavyweight sterling silver with two attractively carved roses, **$85.** (3) Sterling silver ring with paste stones, **$65.** (4) Mother-of-pearl clip-on type earrings, **$15.** (5) Beads, possibly Bohemian. The cranberry-colored oval beads are adhered to a white satin glass back, **$35.** (6) Adjustable ring with a paste amethyst stone in ornate brass setting; from the Roaring Twenties, **$65.** (7) Art Nouveau ring, brass setting, paste turquoise stone, adjustable, **$38.** (8) Ring, aluminum setting, aquamarine paste stone, adjustable, **$35.** (9) Sterling silver ring, paste stones, **$65.** (10) Ring, cinnabar, in an ornate brass setting, adjustable, marked "China," **$75.**

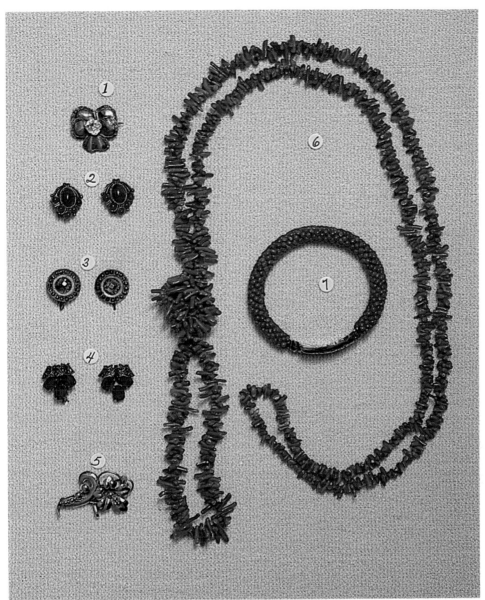

(1) Sterling silver pansy brooch, paste stone, **$65.** (2) Earrings, paste stones, base metal, screw posts, **$22.** (3) Earrings, cut steel riveted on brass, C. 1880, **$35.** (4) Earrings, paste red garnets on oxidized brass filigree, screw posts, made in Czechoslovakia, **$30.** (5) Watch pin, ¹⁄₂₀ of 12 karat gold-filled, **$75.** (6) Beads, real branch coral, 28″ long, **$250.** (7) Bracelet, real coral, **$150.**

(1) Heavyweight sterling silver brooch, **$65.** (2) Hatpin with dangle, white metal set with paste stones, from the 1920s, **$55.** (3) Necklace of lacy silver wire coated to prevent oxidation, paste stones, possibly Mexican, **$65.** (4) Bar pin brooch, paste stones, base metal, **$45.** (5) Brooch, white base metal, paste stones, **$55.** (6) Small, rectangular brooch of white base metal, paste stones, **$25.**

All of the mosaic jewelry pictured, C. 1880-1920. (1) Beautifully executed brooch, has brass back with beaded edge, **$45.** (2) Bracelet with very fine detail on base metal back, beaded edge, **$55.** (3) Brooch, shaped like a safety pin with white metal backing on each drop, very fine mosaic detail, **$55.** (4) Necklace, each bead interspaced with two paste coral beads, knotted, **$175.** (5) Mosaic on goldstone brooch with chain and pin. Can be worn flipped over. Back has a place for photograph or lock of hair. Frame is gold, **$250.** (6) Brooch, musical instrument, mosaic on brass back, **$50.** (7) Bracelet with silver-washed copper links, beaded edges, **$75.**

(1) Screw post earrings, paste stones on base metal, **$22.** (2) Brooch, windmill with movable part, sterling silver, "Lang" hallmark, **$55.** (3) Earrings, celluloid with screw posts, white metal, match beads in center, **$45.** (4) Celluloid earrings, with slide-on celluloid clip (slide-on types are scarce), **$35.** (5) Wreath brooch, oxidized base metal with paste stones, **$45.** (6) Necklace to match No. 3 earrings, celluloid raspberries interspaced with tiny gray beads, strung on thin, cloth covered wire, **$55.** (7) Brooch, wooden bow, Art Deco, **$30.** (8) Heavyweight sterling silver earrings, paste turquoise stones, screw posts, **$65.** (9) Earrings, gold wash over sterling silver, paste turquoise stones, screw posts, **$35.** (10) Peruvian silver brooch, marked "925 pure," heavyweight, **$55.** (11) Earrings, brass, paste stones, **$22.**

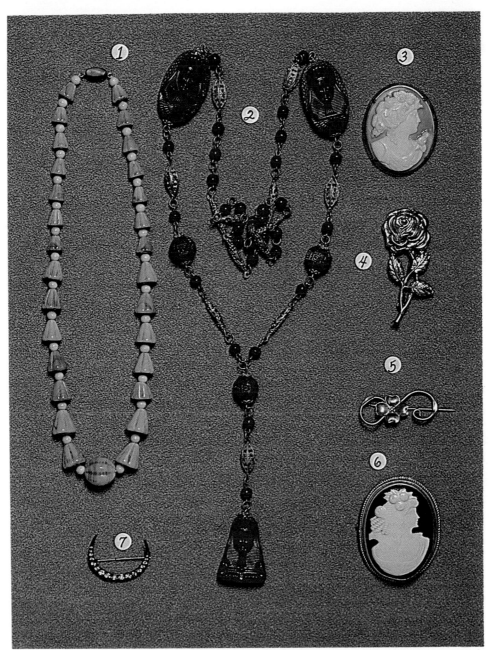

(1) Glass beads, made in Czechoslovakia. Each cone has a brass finding at the bottom of its flat part. These are interspaced with small beads. Matching faceted paste bead on clasp, **$35.** (2) Necklace, red pressed glass, with an oriental woman's face with headdress in relief on large disks. Chain is white metal with brass ornaments, 19″ long, **$125.** (3) Celluloid cameo brooch in gold-washed brass frame, **$85.** (4) Sterling silver rose brooch, **$65.** (5) Brooch, sterling silver, **$45.** (6) Celluloid cameo brooch in white metal frame, **$65.**

(1) Necklace, milk glass, lower six pieces with elephants in relief, **$25.**

(2) Clear pressed glass faceted beads, 24″ long, **$50.**

(3) Beads, choker length, very unusual, pink with satin finish. Filled with a chalklike compound that makes them very light in weight, **$40.**

(4) Necklace, 42″ long, brass beads with white enamel, loop-over style, **$55.**

(5) Art Deco brooch, blue and white enamel on copper, **$65.**

(6) Brooch, base metal with clear glass stones, **$25.**

(7) Brooch, hollowware with gold wash over copper. **$38.**

(8) Brooch, sterling silver violets, with coating to prevent oxidation, **$55.**

(9) Brooch, enamel with blue paste stones, **$28.**

(1) Beads, pressed glass, amber in color with brass filigree spacers, **$55.**

(2) Round, pink glass beads with blue squares and clear flat spacers, **$32.**

(3) Beads, dyed buffalo horn in coral color, **$40.**

(4) Brass necklace with pressed glass beads, **$55.**

(5) Brooch, black celluloid cameo applied to tortoiseshell with oval back, **$65.**

(6) Brooch, grapes and leaf, sterling silver, **$55.**

(7) Brooch, Art Deco, brass and black enamel, **$28.**

(1) Bracelet, gold wash over brass, link chain with two faceted, amber color beads, **$32.**

(2) Arrow brooch, oxidized base metal with paste diamonds, **$35.**

(3) Necklace, oxidized base metal with characteristics of silver, milk glass beads in center of flower, **$45.**

(4) Brooch, gold wash over brass, paste stones with four enameled scrolls, made in Czechoslovakia, **$30.**

(5) Brooch, girl reading book, oxidized base metal with a thin wash of silver, **$35.**

(6) Brooch, flying insect, gold wash over brass, made in Czechoslovakia, **$40.**

(7) Beads, choker length, early plastic, **$40.**

(8) Brooch, oxidized base metal with imitation red stones, **$45.**

(9) Brooch, sterling silver, flowers tied with bow, **$35.**

(10) Brooch, base metal with characteristics of silver. Blue imitation moonstones with imitation diamonds. Edges of leaves and stem are blue enamel, **$55.**

(11) Necklace, red celluloid. Lower half has four strands of lacy cutouts, **$65.**

(1) Beads, black glass, 27″ long, **$65.**

(2) Beads, 15″ long, pressed crystal, with two clear spacers on each side of the flat amethyst disks, **$60.**

(3) Brooch, three violets, sterling silver, **$55.**

(4) Brooch, brass, center is early plastic and orange in color, **$28.**

(5) Brooch, base metal with characteristics of silver, **$22.**

(6) Lavaliere, pressed composition beads and drop. Chain is brass. The six large, round, tubular beads have a flat brass disk at each side, **$75.**

(7) Brooch, Republican elephant, in cloisonné on copper, **$45.**

(8) Brooch, celluloid cameo set in brass enameled frame. Beautiful high relief; an early piece, **$55.**

(9) Cameo, white pressed celluloid applied to navy blue back. Set in a brass gilt frame, **$50.**

(10) Brooch, large imitation garnet in scroll frame of gold wash over brass. A thin gold piece pierces through the scroll frame, **$65.**

(1) Necklace, old inlaid turquoise from India, **$95.**

(2) Brooch, with imitation pearls and turquoise, gold washed brass frame, **$22.**

(3) Brooch, with gold top applied over brass, **$28.**

(4) Lavaliere, paste beads are dark garnet color. Stones set in gold washed brass. Chain also gold washed, **$85.**

(5) Necklace, flowers are made of thin metal, silver wash. The green stones in the center are paste, **$55.**

(6) Brooch, cloisonné on copper, **$38.**

(7) Bracelet, Art Deco, with blue and clear paste stones set in chrome, **$95.**

(8) Earrings, red paste stones set in sterling silver with screw posts, **$65.**

(9) Earrings, sterling silver, screw posts, **$35.**

(10) Earrings, silver washed base metal, twin acorns and leaves. Early clip-on type, **$45.**

(11) Bar pin, sterling silver with green and crystal paste stones, **$55.**

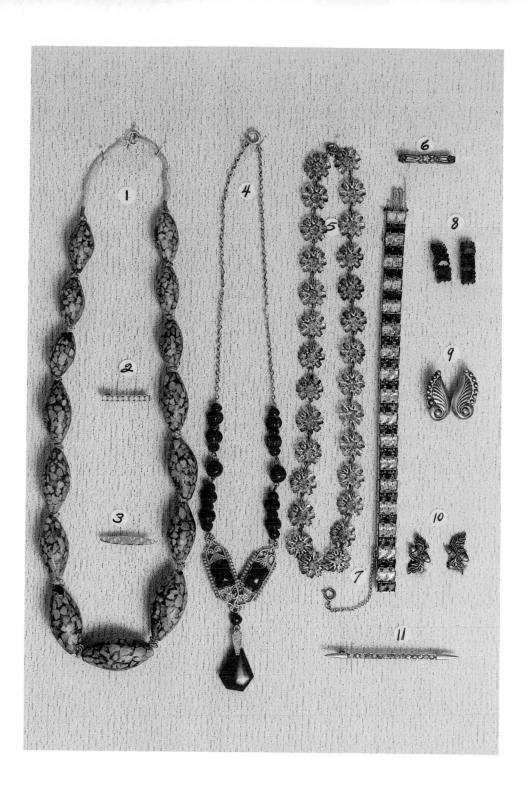

(1) Necklace, imitation pearls, **$35.**

(2) Necklace, gold wash over brass. Center of bow lifts to unhook, **$32.**

(3) Brooch, milk glass cameo of Indian woman, set in a frame of gold wash over brass, **$85.**

(4) Lavaliere, with pearl pendant and teardrop of imitation baroque pearls set in ornate, gold washed frame, **$35.**

(5) Necklace, carved ivory with crystal spacers, **$85.**

(6) Necklace, imitation moonstones on low karat gold chain. Pendant is of feldspar and has a peephole for viewing pictures inside, **$65.**

(7) Butterfly and flower brooch, cloisonné on copper, **$65.**

(8) Letter U brooch, gold wash over copper, **$20.**

(9) Buckle, three-piece, all stones imitation, set in characteristics of silver metal. The stones are beautiful pink and pale amethysts. Tiny rhinestones border the edge, **$95.**

(10) Cameo, high relief, set in gold plated frame, **$85.**

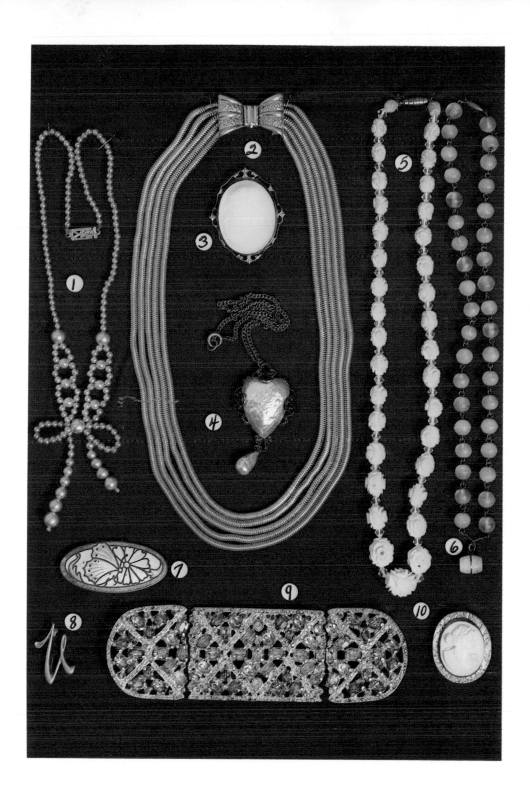

(1) Brooch, red plastic bow, late 1930s, **$18.**

(2) Bracelet, enamel and paste lapis lazuli, gold wash over brass, Art Deco, **$85.**

(3) Brooch, sterling silver poppy, **$65.**

(4) Brooch, oxidized base metal with blue paste stones, **$55.**

(5) Brooch, inlaid bits of turquoise in base metal frame, from India, **$45.**

(6) Necklace, Art Deco, graduated beads of black pressed glass spaced with small beads. Notice the beautiful glass screw fastener. A rare find, **$95.**

(7) Earrings, matching No. 6, above. Screw posts, **$55.**

(8) Flower brooch, base metal with enameled stem and leaves. Although the enamel on the stem is worn, the piece is included because of its beauty. If perfect, **$45.**

(9) Pendant, cameo and chain are celluloid. Notice the fastener, **$75.**

(10) Bracelet, oxidized base metal with blue paste stones. This bracelet and brooch (No. 4) are not part of a set. The two pieces are different shades of blue, **$65.**

(11) Brooch, sterling silver, early piece, **$55.**

(1) Brooch, gold-washed frame with design on celluloid, **$38.**

(2) Brooch, rose design under glass, gold-washed, **$32.**

(3) Clip, paste turquoise in oxidized brass frame, **$55.**

(4) Carved ivory brooch, **$65.**

(5) Necklace, celluloid chain and flower, **$58.**

(6) Bracelet to match No. 5, **$55.**

(7) Scarf pin, gold plate; both ends open from the center, **$35.**

(8) Brooch, carved bow in mother-of-pearl, **$28.**

(9) Brooch, buckle-shaped, of carved pearl, **$30.**

(10) Brooch flower holder with spring fastener, **$65.**

(11) Watchband of imitation pearls, **$75.**

(12) Small bar pin, gold plate, **$28.**

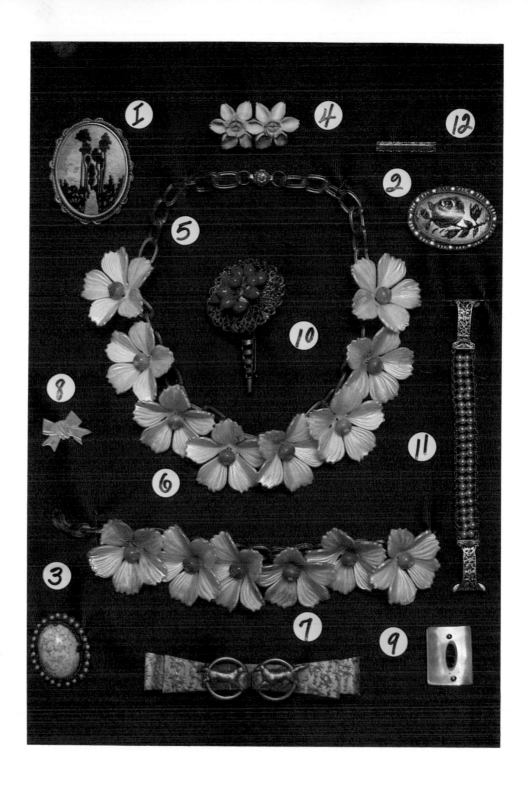

(1) Mosaic earrings, with screw backs, **$50.**

(2) Oval mosaic earrings, rare, **$75.**

(3) Horse's head earrings, sterling silver, **$42.**

(4) Earrings, paste turquoise set in sterling silver, **$48.**

(5) Clip, kaleidoscope effect, **$45.**

(6) Blue bird brooch, enamel, **$58.**

(7) Necklace, black paste in brass drops, **$55.**

(8) Brooch, to match No. 7, **$45.**

(9) Cameo pin, celluloid in gold-washed frame, **$75.**

(10) Cloverleaf earrings, abalone set in sterling silver, **$75.**

(11) Sterling silver earrings, bows, with paste amethyst stones, **$65.**

(12) Celluloid cameo, in gold-washed frame; rare in this tiny size, **$55.**

(13) English sterling silver locket, **$65.**

(14) Cameo, pressed milk glass in gold-washed frame, **$85.**

(15) Locket, oxidized brass, **$45.**

(1) Brooch, paste stone flowers in basket, **$32.**

(2) Flag pin, enameled on sterling silver, **$65.**

(3) Heart-shaped brooch, pearl shell in gold-washed frame, **$32.**

(4) Brooch of paste amethysts, gold plated, **$55.**

(5) Pale blue bead choker, hand-painted flowers on beads, **$55.**

(6) Small bar pin, with paste stones set in sterling silver, **$48.**

(7) Gold-plated bar pin with tiny seed pearls, **$55.**

(8) Gold pin, textured gold motif and blue enameled flowers, **$22.**

(9) Brooch, branches of berries and leaves, gold-washed, **$38.**

(10) Brooch, colored paste stones, enameled flowers and leaves on base metal, **$55.**

(11) Brooch, lilies, silver on copper, **$45.**

(12) Watch pin, gold plated, **$65.**

(13) Bar pin, enamel on copper, **$38.**

(14) Sterling silver brooch, paste stones, **$75.**

(15) Brooch, buckle-shaped, gold-washed, **$48.**

(1) Choker length beads, milk glass, unusual, **$30.**

(2) Necklace, celluloid, coral, and turquoise, screw fastener, **$48.**

(3) Brooch, round plain disk of pearl, **$10.**

(4) Beads, cranberry color with clear spacers. Cranberry beads are rare, **$75.**

(5) Art Deco beads. Large bead pencil striped in black enamel. Other beads are five-sided. Smaller beads have three cutouts on each edge, are spaced with large and small faceted round beads, **$65.**

(6) Cuff links, silver-plated with paste turquoise, **$38.**

(7) Cuff links, Masonic, sterling silver, **$65.**

(8) Art Deco sterling silver dogwood flower brooch, **$50.**

(9) Brooch in sterling silver has been coated to prevent oxidation. Heavyweight, **$85.**

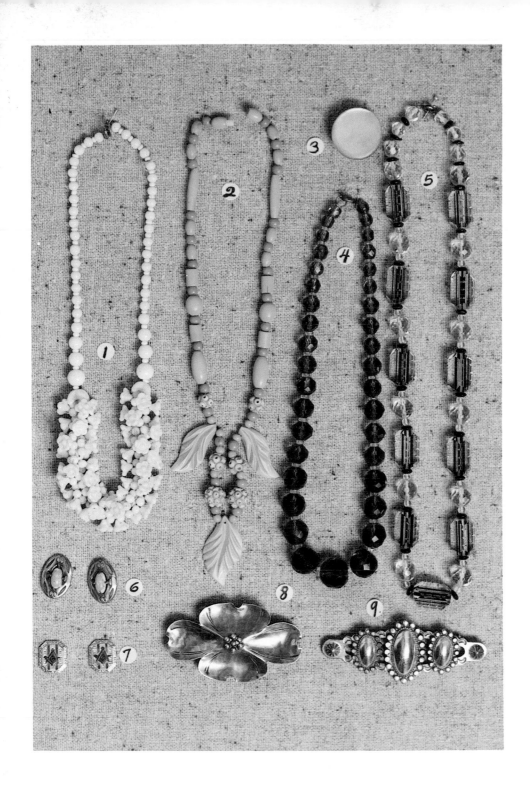

(1) Unusual charm necklace, all brass, **$95.**

(2) Buckle brooch, gold-washed with paste stones, **$58.**

(3) Button-type brooch, with paste stones in sterling silver setting, **$65.**

(4) Cloverleaf pin, green abalone set in sterling silver, **$75.**

(5) Cloisonné bar pin, **$48.**

(6) Mosaic dragonfly brooch. Wings on dragonfly have colors similar to those found on Tiffany peacock lampshades. Price depends upon how skillfully the piece is executed, **$85.**

(7) Mosaic brooch, **$55.**

(8) Unusual sterling silver brooch, **$65.**

(9) Large brooch, of paste stones set in oxidized silver, **$38.**

(10) Large lacy brooch, brass, **$20.**

(11) Brooch, with paste center stone, enameled leaf on each corner, **$38.**

(12) Bar pin, gold-washed with paste acorn, **$45.**

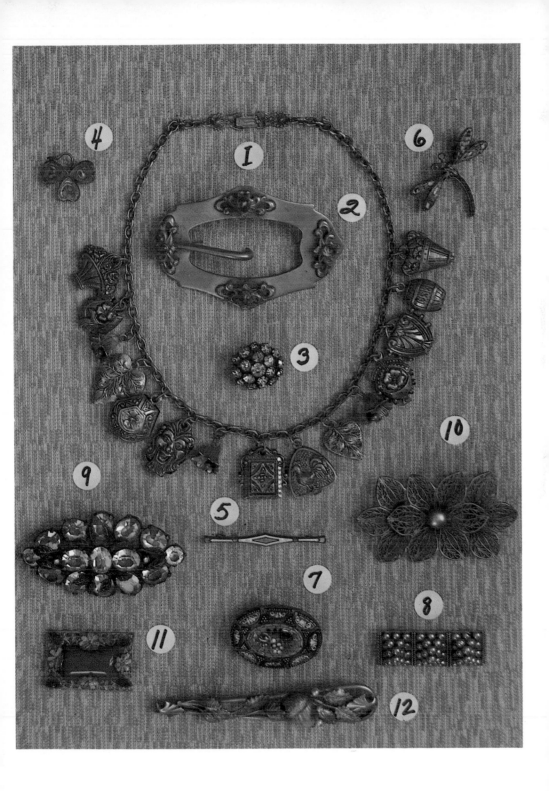

(1) Earrings, base metal, imitation stones, Art Deco, **$45.**

(2) Brooch, wheat design in imitation pearl, brass frame, **$28.**

(3) Brooch, branch of coral, celluloid, **$25.**

(4) Brooch, heavyweight sterling silver, **$40.**

(5) Beads, pressed faceted crystal, **$28.**

(6) Butterfly, made of aluminum. Wings have small applied ornaments, **$35.**

(7) Brooch, base metal with silver wash, imitation stone, **$28.**

(8) Elephant, has a loop for a chain, celluloid, **$32.**

(9) Bracelet, carved ivory, flower centers are tinted, **$95.**

(10) Necklace, cut crystal, **$42.**

(11) Bracelet, enamel on iron, probably from Germany, **$28.**

(12) Brooch, paste stone citrine in base metal frame, **$22.**

(1) Beads, aqua color, on chain, 14″ long, **$75.**

(2) Dark brown beads with light blue foil effect, probably Venetian glass, 17″ long, **$95.**

(3) Brooch, ribbon with buckle, paste stone, gold-washed, **$65.**

(4) Brooch, coral-colored celluloid. This was reproduced in the 1960s, **$55.**

(5) Sterling silver violin, hallmarked, **$75.**

(6) Brooch, rose transfer on mother-of-pearl under glass, in gold frame, **$85.**

(7) Cameo, black pressed glass, **$30.**

(8) Brooch, paste stones in gold-washed frame, **$28.**

(9) Brooch, coral-colored celluloid, **$65.**

(10) Horseshoe brooch with paste amethysts, **$45.**

(11) Clip, pink and amethyst paste stones, **$65.**

(12) Enameled brooch, ribbon and bow on base metal, **$28.**

(13) Bar pin, paste stones in heavy brass frame, **$28.**

(14) Locket, stamp engraved front and back, applied cameo, gold-washed, **$38.**

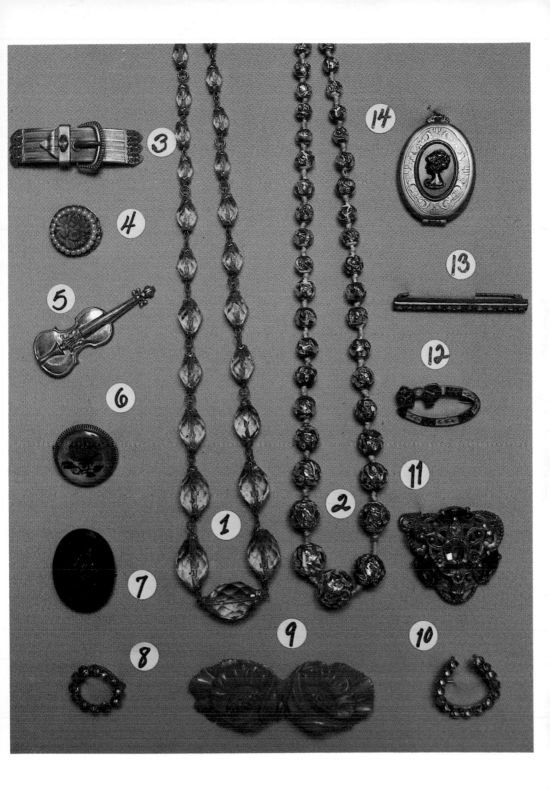

(1) Gold filigree sunflower brooch, **$85.**

(2) Enameled bluebird stickpin, **$65.**

(3) Sterling silver bar pin, hand-painted roses and leaves, **$28.**

(4) Brooch, silver effect on base metal, **$10.**

(5) This pin is brass with a satin finish that is burnished at the high points. Set with paste amethyst stone. A brooch in this particular finish is seldom found, **$55.**

(6) Sterling silver brooch, Art Deco, **$32.**

(7) Brooch, Art Nouveau, pond lilies and paste stones, **$35.**

(8) Brooch, silver-type base metal, **$12.**

(9) Brooch, silver-washed, with a protective film over the enameled clover leaves, **$24.**

(10) Brooch, enamel on gold, **$85.**

(11) Brooch, cinnabar, marked "China," **$65.**

(12) Brooch, paste stones, made during 1920s, **$45.**

(13) Necklace of birds and pink-colored paste stones, **$45.**

(14) Brooch, heavy sterling silver marked "800 fine," with a pullout spring fastener, **$120.**

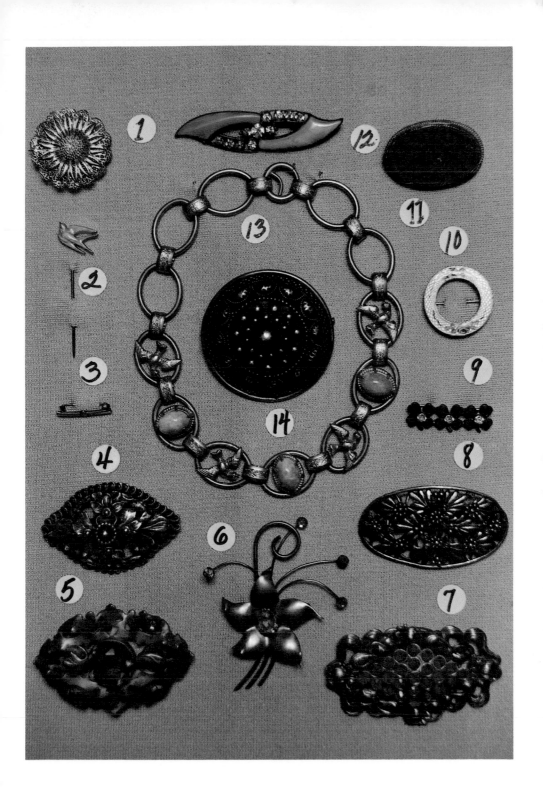

(1) Very attractive glass beads remind one of agate, **$65.**

(2) Stickpin, gold-washed. Pansy has a turquoise in center, **$35.**

(3) Bar pin, sterling silver, **$55.**

(4) Art Nouveau brooch, gold-washed with paste stone, **$75.**

(5) Beads, 21″ long, **$95.**

(6) Beads with overlay decoration, may be Venetian, **$120.**

(7) Brooch, gold-washed with half pearls, **$65.**

(8) Brooch, gold-washed lace filigree with paste stone, **$45.**

(9) Bracelet, flexible band with adjustable slide and paste stones, **$95.**

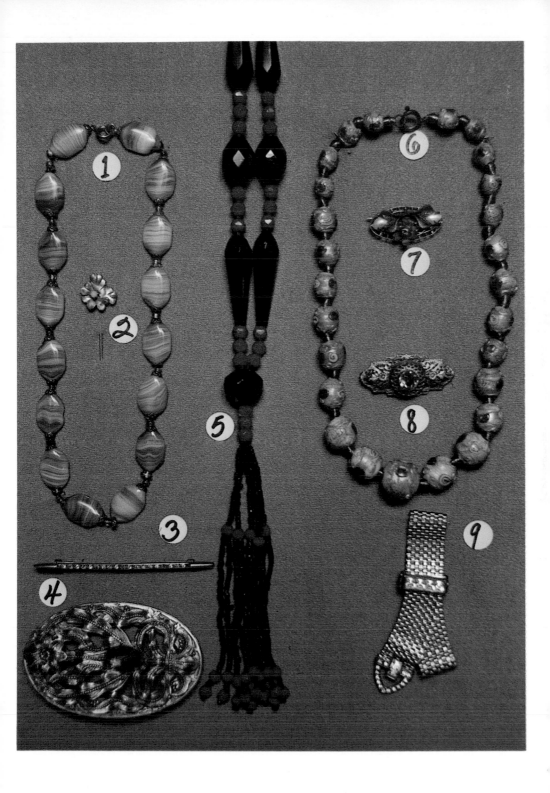

(1) Brooch, roses, sterling silver, **$75.**

(2) Celluloid brooch, **$65**

(3) Wild rose brooch, sterling silver, **$45.**

(4) Brooch, Art Nouveau, brass flower, **$25.**

(5) Brooch, Art Nouveau, woman with flowing hair on lily pad, **$45.**

(6) Brooch, sterling silver filigree, **$65.**

(7) Cameo, pressed glass, marked "Czechoslovakia," **$30.**

(8) Brooch, bell-shaped flowers, sterling silver, **$45.**

(9) Cameo, celluloid on black glass in gold-washed frame, **$60.**

(10) Brooch, silver effect with filigreed ball in center, **$25.**

(11) Glass beads, ruby color; drop has oxidized brass ornament; 20″ long, **$95.**

(12) Beads, pale blue on silver-type chain 19″ long, **$95.**

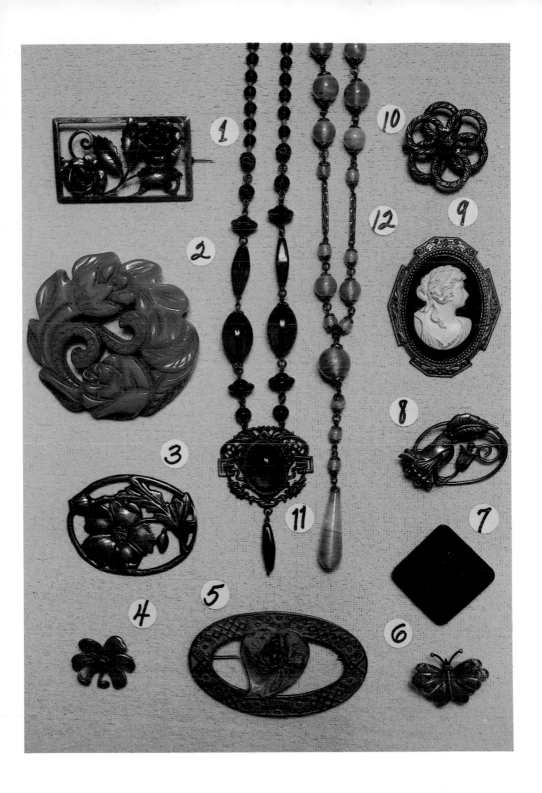

(1) Blue spatter glass beads, screw fastener, **$65.**

(2) Necklace, paste turquoise in oxidized metal frame, **$32.**

(3) Beads, celluloid, very unusual, **$68.**

(4) Mosaic bracelet, very fine work, **$85.**

(5) Brooch, bird enameled on brass. For collectors of birds this is a find, **$75.**

(6) Brooch, bird in a cage, sterling silver with plate hallmarked "Lang," **$45.**

(7) Brooch, paste stone in a gold-washed frame, **$22.**

(8) Cameo, in gold-washed, openwork frame, **$75.**

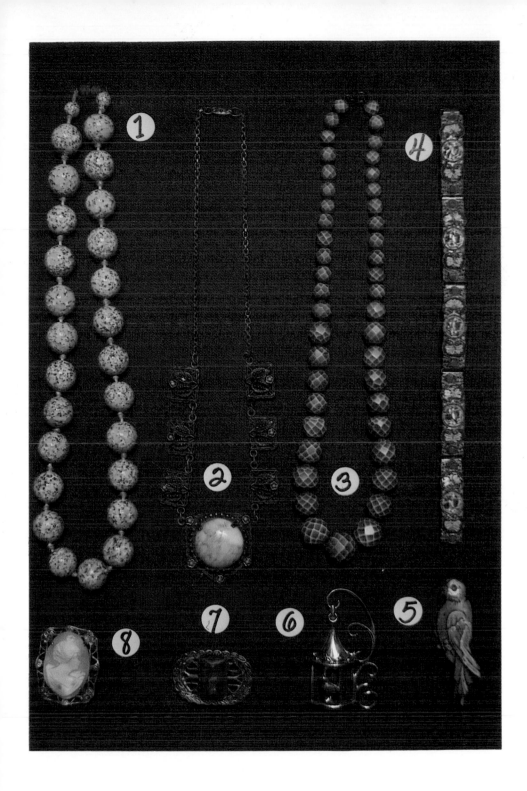

(1) Bracelet, base metal opens on side, filigreed top with blue imitation moonstones, **$55.**

(2) Bracelet, heavy braided base metal, open center back, slip-on type, **$28.**

(3) Bangle, sterling silver, **$45.**

(4) Bangle, silver gilt over brass, imitation diamonds, **$28.**

(5) Bangle, thin, gold plate over copper, stamped design, **$48.**

(6) Bracelet, silver plate over base metal; top design in repoussé. Has side clasp, **$35.**

(7) Bangle, sterling silver with Indian portrait was sold as souvenir at the Mohawk Trail souvenir shops in New York State, **$75.**

(8) Bangle, heavyweight sterling silver with turquoise, **$95.**

(9) Bangle, carved celluloid, **$48.**

(10) Bangle, slip-on type, sterling silver with imitation turquoise; American Indian design, **$75.**

(11) Bangle, yellow brass filigree band with applied top. Slip-on type, **$30.**

(12) Bangle, sterling silver raised flowers and leaves, slip-on type, **$85.**

(13) Bangle, early plastic blue and white imitation stones, **$95.**

(14) French jet beads on brass coil, **$55.**

1

6

11

7

2

12

3

8

4

13

9

5

10

14

(1) Earrings, sterling silver American Indian design, screw posts, **$65.**

(2) Ring, characteristics of silver, citrine paste stones, **$28.**

(3) Butterfly, colored paste stones on base metal, **$35.**

(4) Brooch, cloisonné on copper, **$75.**

(5) Buckle, two piece, centers are paste pearls set in chrome, **$25.**

(6) Necklace, cut crystals set in brass chain. Signed "Fischer" on the snap clasp, **$95.**

(7) Dog brooch, American Indian design, sterling silver, **$100.**

(8) Brooch, Mexican with two buckets, marked "Silver Mexico," **$85.**

(9) Lavaliere, sterling silver, poppies, has loop for a chain, **$65.**

(10) Ring, characteristics of silver, black paste stone, **$30.**

(11) Brooch, base metal with gold wash, blue paste stone, **$25.**

(1) Cameo, milk glass set in a gold-washed frame, **$65.**

(2) Bar pin, some parts are enameled; silver wash over copper, **$32.**

(3) Large pin can be worn as a lavaliere by threading a chain through hinged eyelet on back. Flower top lifts up to receive a cake of perfume. Scent escapes through holes in back. A collector's delight, **$30.**

(4) Brooch, brass filigree center with red beads, **$32.**

(5) Brooch with green paste stone, **$35.**

(6) Bar pin, gold-washed with paste stones, **$38.**

(7) Brooch, enameled leaves and imitation pearls, **$40.**

(8) Brooch, paste stone in a gold-washed frame, **$30.**

(9) Brooch, paste topaz in a gold-washed frame, **$32.**

(10) Brooch, paste stones in an oxidized, base metal frame, **$55.**

(11) Cameo, brown celluloid on ivory, **$50.**

(12) Brooch, carved ebony, **$65.**

(13) Beads, white with red polka dots, 16″ long, **$75.**

(14) Necklace, paste stones set in silver-type base metal frame that is engraved on back, **$55.**

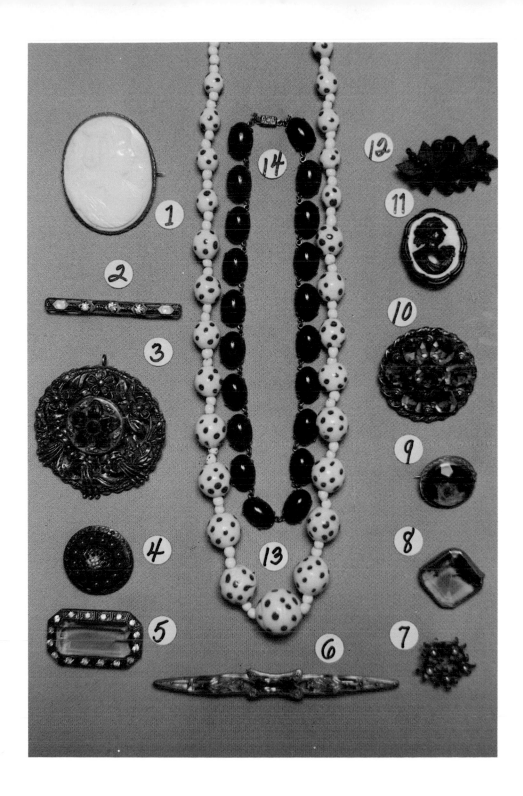

(1) Beads, celluloid and white milk glass. The two lower white beads have impressed elephants, **$55.**

(2) Chatelaine charm, base metal, except the part from which the charms hang which is sterling, **$45.**

(3) Glass beads spaced with plain and filigreed brass beads, **$65.**

(4) Brooch, brass topped with applied thin gold piece, **$25.**

(5) Brooch, characteristics of silver, with clear paste stones and center pink imitation moonstone, **$55.**

(6) Beads, amber-colored paste with conical satin glass spacers, **$48.**

(7) Locket, gold plate with imitation diamonds, **$95.**

(8) Pin, Art Deco, enamel on copper, **$28.**

(9) Buckle, two piece plastic, early 1930s, **$28.**

71

(1) Art Deco sterling silver bracelet, **$90.**

(2) Bracelet, sterling silver with enamel, **$95.**

(3) Heavy bracelet, sterling silver with flowers, **$80.**

(4) Bracelet, sterling silver, rope twist, **$75.**

(5) Bracelet, silver plate; flowers are gardenias, **$45.**

(6) Wooden beads with screw fasteners, **$55.**

(7) Brooch, wreath-shaped in sterling silver, **$35.**

(8) Brooch, stork in the rushes, heavy sterling silver, **$55.**

(9) Brooch, horse's head in sterling silver, **$45.**

(10) Charm bracelet, C. 1910-1920, base metal, **$45.**

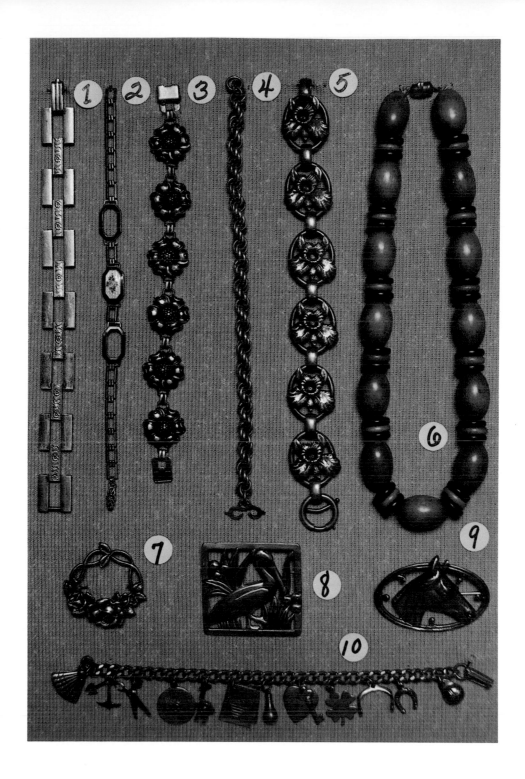

(1) Bracelet, silver on copper. Lilies of the valley in high relief. Silver slightly worn, which adds to its beauty, **$55.**

(2) Bar pin, with paste stone, unusual, **$35.**

(3) Large brooch to match No. 1, beautiful relief, **$45.**

(4) Brooch, silver-washed over copper with black enameled leaves, paste stones, **$20.**

(5) Rooster brooch, Art Nouveau, all enameled, high relief, **$65.**

(6) Paste beads, unusual, resembling light blue ice crystals, **$55.**

(7) Necklace, filigreed brass chain with paste stones set in full back frame, **$75.**

(8) Turtle brooch, sterling silver, **$35.**

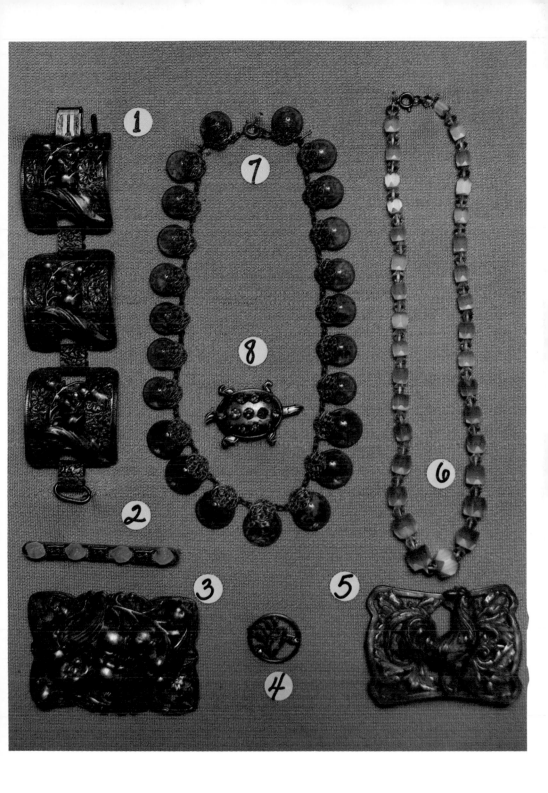

(1) Necklace, flat openwork, engraved brass chain with amethyst paste stones, **$75.**

(2) Beads. Sometimes sold for real coral, these are actually pressed celluloid, 14½″ long, **$65.**

(3) Brooch, engraved design on oxidized brass, with six rhinestones, pinkish coral paste stone in center, **$75.**

(4) Beads, pale, opaque blue, **$45.**

(5) Brooch, Art Nouveau, heavy sterling silver flower, **$75.**

(6) Tiny jackknife, abalone, **$50.**

(7) Necklace, paste amethyst, rose pressed stone, **$85.**

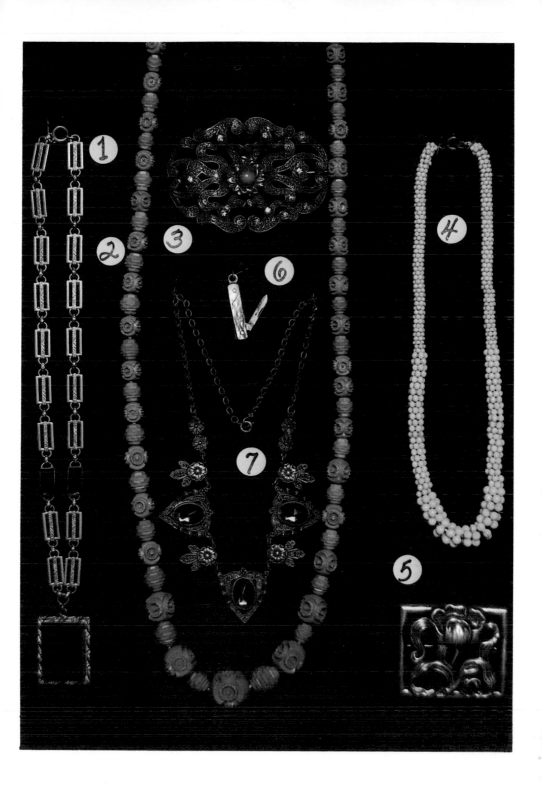

(1) Beads, blue glass resembling lapis lazuli, silver disks on a chain, screw fastener, **$75.**

(2) Beads, knotted, amethyst color, 15″ long, **$75.**

(3) Brooch, Art Nouveau, woman's bust, enameled leaves, sterling silver, **$95.**

(4) Butterfly brooch, black glass on metal, **$45.**

(5) Lavaliere, paste onyx and small marcasites in center set in a solid-backed sterling silver frame, **$75.**

(6) Lovebird necklace, paste topaz stones, **$55.**

(7) Pin, three link, gold-washed, **$18.**

(8) Small gold bar pin, **$55.**

(9) Brooch, sterling silver filigree, **$65.**

(10) Cloisonné brooch, **$75.**

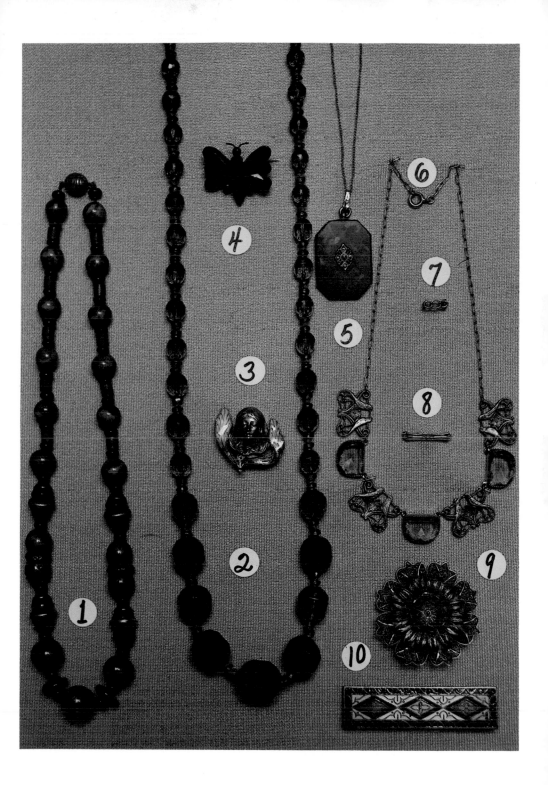

(1) Ring, paste stone set flush in sterling silver mounting, **$65.**

(2) Ring, paste stones, rolled gold, **$38.**

(3) Ring, blue paste stone in a basket setting, has characteristics of silver, **$28.**

(4) Ring, with heart-shaped stone, gold filled, **$48.**

(5) Ring, scarab in unusual setting, hallmark under setting and on outside band; sterling silver, **$85.**

(6) Ring, characteristics of silver, paste stone. Now a collectible, **$18.**

(7) Ring, gold-washed, paste stone, marked "Made in U.S.A.," **$22.**

(8) Ring, man's sterling silver, initialed, **$50.**

(9) Ring, 10 karat gold-filled, **$65.**

(10) Ring, silver-washed on brass. Adjustable band with a beautiful imitation fire opal. Probably Czechoslovakian, **$55.**

(11) Ring, silver-washed over brass, **$38.**

(12) Ring, sterling silver basket setting. Paste stone in lovely amethyst color, **$75.**

(13) Ring, rose pressed paste onyx in sterling silver, **$45.**

(14) Ring, Art Deco, sterling silver, paste stones, **$45.**

(15) Ring, heart-shaped, 10 karat gold, **$65.**

(16) Ring, paste stone, gold-washed brass, beautiful work, **$48.**

(17) Necklace, gold plated, **$35.**

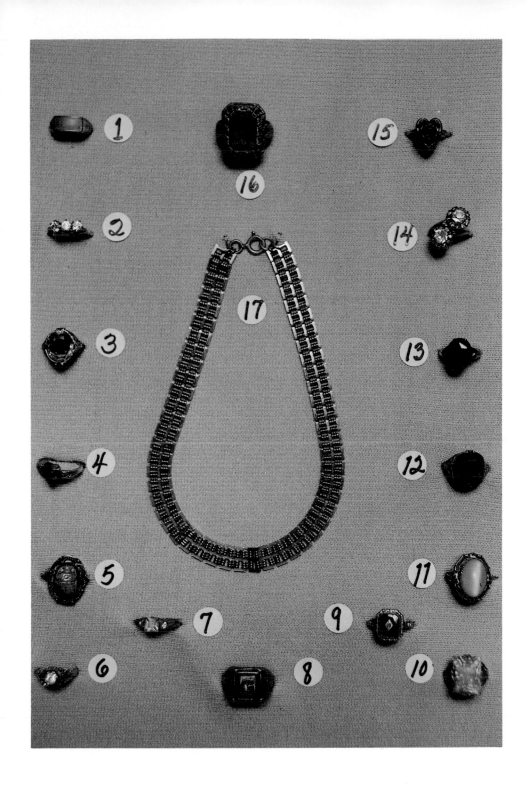

(1) Brooch, intaglio cut, hand painted, gold-washed frame, **$55.**

(2) Brooch, carved bone, **$85.**

(3) Butterfly, made C. 1920, has been reproduced, **$45.**

(4) Bracelet of imitation pearls, made C. 1920, **$55.**

(5) Bracelet, sterling silver, beautiful relief, **$75.**

(6) Bracelet, link band with paste stones, **$75.**

(7) Bracelet, sterling silver with paste moonstones, **$85.**

(8) Lovely turn-of-the century bracelet, **$65.**

(9) Bracelet, paste stone, gold-washed over sterling silver, **$75.**

(10) Bracelet, flexible, enameled band, **$65.**

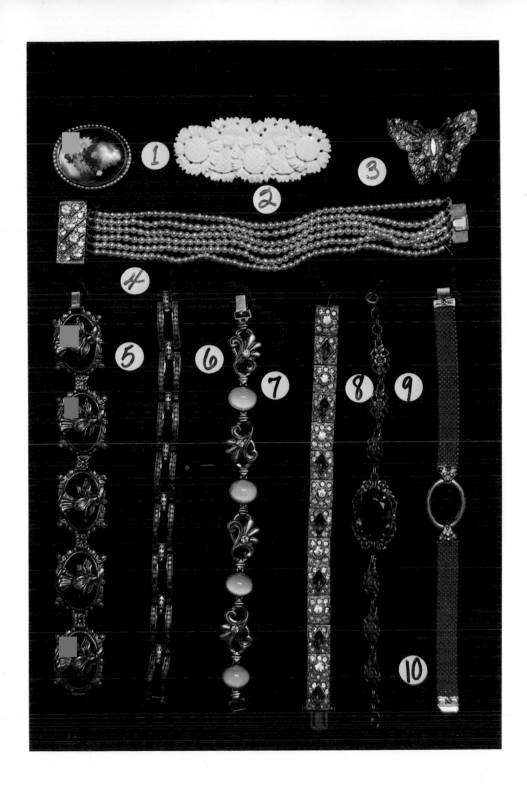

(1) Carved ebony cross topped with a celluloid cross. Chain is celluloid. Notice hook, **$100.**

(2) Brooch, seahorse, sterling silver, **$75.**

(3) Necklace, beaded, crocheted, **$65.**

(4) Beads, real jet, **$95.**

(5) Earrings, black glass. Design on the drops is adhered to base metal. Posts also base metal, **$45.**

(1) Flexible bracelet characteristics of silver, paste stones, **$45.**

(2) Wild rose, brooch, gold-washed, **$25.**

(3) Crescent brooch, paste amethyst stones in sterling silver frame, **$48.**

(4) Brooch, gold-washed, paste stones, **$28.**

(5) Brooch, rose on arrow, base metal, **$22.**

(6) Necklace, heavy sterling silver chain, horseshoe with paste drop, **$85.**

(7) Bracelet to match No. 6, **$65.**

(8) Brooch, colored paste stones in a base metal frame, **$28.**

(9) Earrings, bunches of grapes, sterling silver with hallmark, **$38.**

(10) Brooch, Indian in dress, turquoise stone, **$55.**

(11) Brooch, sterling silver, **$38.**

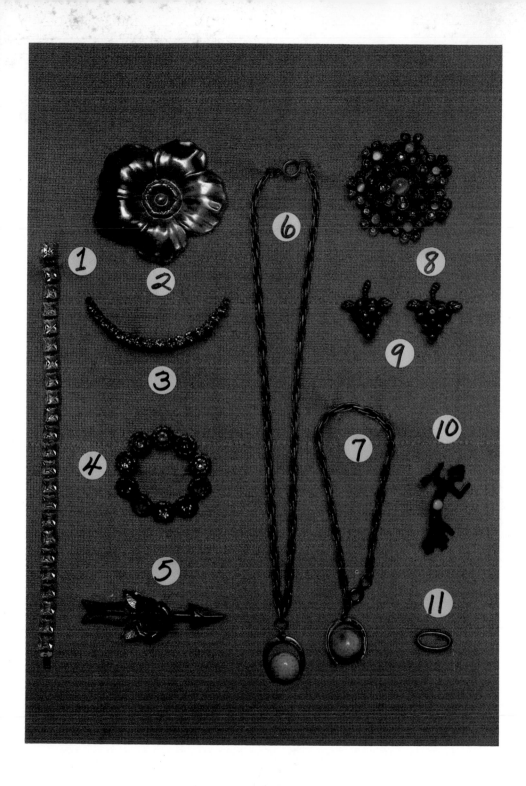

(1) Celluloid beads interspaced with glass beads, **$65.**

(2) Matchstick beads and beautiful imitation turquoise, **$65.**

(3) Joint beads (each falls into the groove of the next), **$55.**

(4) Heart brooch, enamel on brass, **$65.**

(5) Pin, impressed brass, **$45.**

(6) Brooch, enameled maple leaves with paste stones, **$38.**

(7) Thistle brooch, gold-washed and enameled, **$65.**

(8) Cameo set in gold-plated frame, **$55.**

(9) Bar pin, gold-washed with paste amethysts, **$48.**

(10) Brooch, cloisonné, gold-washed, probably European, unusual, **$55.**

(11) Brooch, enamel on sterling silver, **$85.**

(1) Glass beads with milk glass spacers, C. 1920, **$45.**

(2) Lavaliere bow, gold wash over brass, paste stones, **$65.**

(3) Ring, stamp engraved on three sides, high setting with blue imitation stone. Gold wash over brass, **$65.**

(4) Necklace, gold wash over brass and copper, red imitation stones, **$55.**

(5) Locket, gold wash over brass. Horse's head in relief, **$48.**

(6) Beads, early plastic, **$45.**

(7) Necklace, sterling silver with pink quartz drop, **$65.**

(8) Brooch, American Indian, sterling silver. Indian mark on reverse, **$100.**

(9) Brooch, American Indian thunderbird, sterling silver, **$75.**

(10) Brooch, Art Nouveau, gold wash over base metal, **$45.**

(11) Fob, gold plated, dolphin in relief, **$65.**

(12) Brooch, all brass with imitation pearl, **$28.**

(1) Necklace, black glass beads, chain and spirals are one-twentieth of ten karat gold filled, **$75.** (2) Necklace, garnet-colored paste beads; top adhered to satin glass back. Tiny beads are brass; an unusual piece, **$85.** (3) Beads, lemon colored glass with swirl effect, on a base metal chain, **$95.** (4) Pin, gold wash openwork, imitation diamonds, **$40.** (5) Ring, sterling silver with marcasites, **$75.** (6) Pendant, glass beads with imitation stones on brass chain, **$80.** (7) Brooch, clover leaves, paste stones, gold wash frame, **$45.** (8) Charm bracelet, with chain in gilt silver over brass; charms in base metal, **$18.**

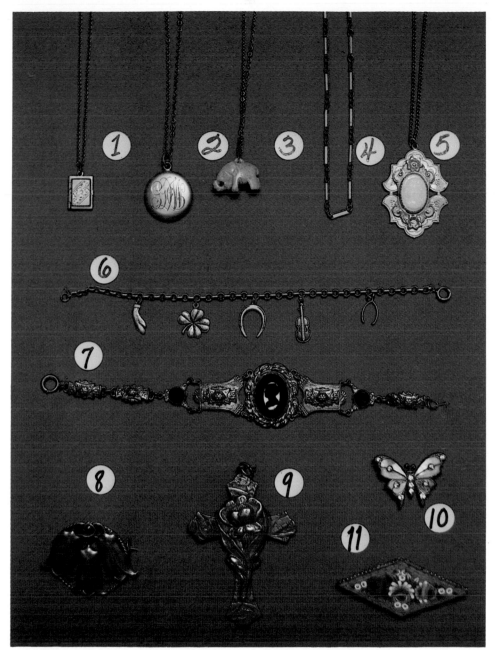

(1) Locket, gold-washed book, **$28.** (2) Locket, satin gold finish. One side initialed; other has tiny diamond, **$95.** (3) Carved jade elephant on chain, **$95.** (4) Chain, enameled, 9″ long, **$85.** (5) Lavaliere, gold-washed, with milk glass cameo, **$65.** (6) Charm bracelet, sterling silver, **$55.** (7) Silhouette bracelet, gold-washed, **$85.** (8) Brooch, bellflowers, sterling silver, **$45.** (9) Cross, silver plated, Art Nouveau, **$50.** (10) Mother-of-pearl butterfly, paste stones, **$45.** (11) Mosaic brooch in a diamond shape, **$45.**

(1) Necklace, green cut crystal, spaced with tiny round beads on upper parts, **$65.** (2) Beads, each round paste bead capped with silver type decorative findings. Chain is brass, **$55.** (3) Necklace, brass and blue glass beads, ornate chain, brass frame, **$85.** (4) Glass beads, melon-shaped with threadings of goldstone; brass findings on each side interspaced with a small flat rosette, **$65.** (5) Bracelet, inlaid with turquoise. This is an old piece from India, **$60.** (6) Earrings, sterling silver, gold wash. Clover has paste garnet, **$55.**

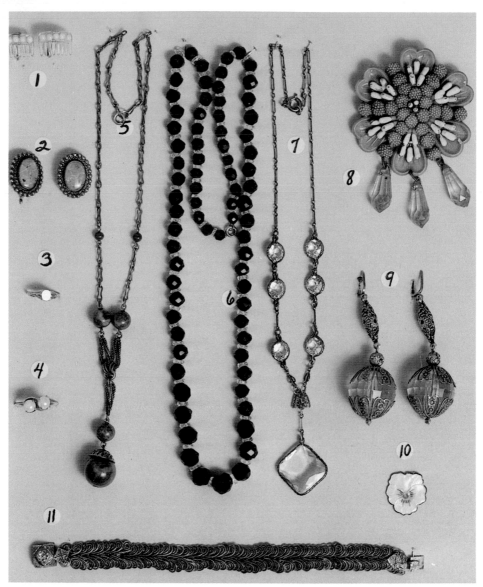

(1) Earrings, celluloid in form of combs, with celluloid posts, **$38.** (2) Earrings, turquoise in sterling silver, **$85.** (3) Baby ring, gold plated, **$32.** (4) Ring, imitation pearls, gold plated, **$55.** (5) Necklace, imitation lapis lazuli, silver plated chain, **$75.** (6) Beads, imitation garnets of early plastic, probably Bakelite, with clear spacers. Ten karat gold clasp, **$75.** (7) Lavaliere, pressed glass crystals set in silver gilt base metal. Chain also silver gilt base metal, **$65.** (8) Celluloid brooch with three paste drops, **$28.** (9) Very unusual and beautiful earrings, screw posts with filigreed brass ornamentation. Balls are early clear plastic. A ½″ brass drop hangs from each. These are C. 1920, **$75.** (10) Pin, pansy enameled on sterling silver, **$75.** (11) Bracelet, flexible sterling silver spirals. Each one is separately joined, **$95.**

(1) Necklace, paste stones, characteristics of sterling silver, **$55.**

(2) Brooch, sterling silver, mermaid plucking a sea flower, **$45.**

(3) Necklace, amber drop, oval amber beads. Black and topaz beads are cut. All paste, 12″ long, **$75.**

(4) Necklace, paste, gold-washed, unusual spool fastener, **$65.**

(5) Beads, ruby color with filigreed beads and long disks on chain, 19½″ long, **$85.**

(6) Necklace, paste stones, base metal with silver-washed, filigree design, **$75.**

(7) Lizard brooch of heavy sterling silver, **$85.**

(8) Brooch, sterling silver bee, beautiful detail, **$55.**

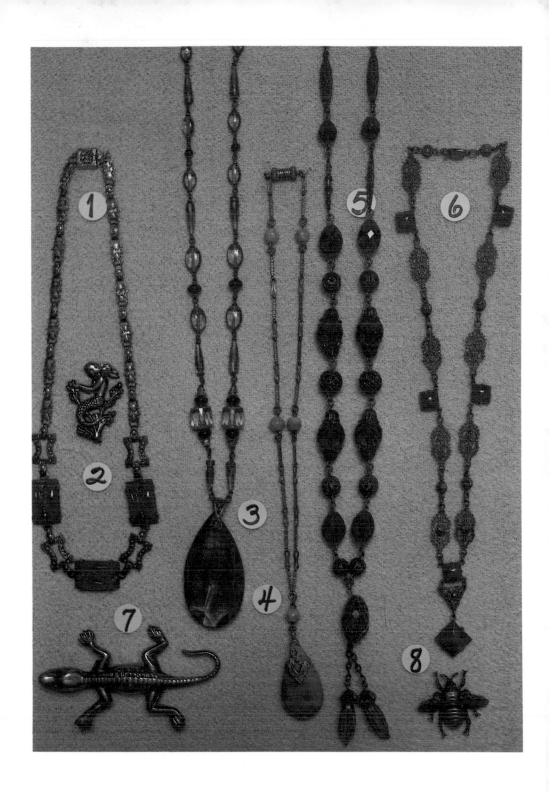

(1) Earrings, all brass including posts. Glass grapes and leaves. These are very scarce, **$75.**

(2) Ring, imitation stones, one-twentieth of twelve karat gold filled, **$60.**

(3) Earrings, cherubs, solid sterling silver, screw posts, **$65.**

(4) Earrings, in base metal with characteristics of silver, **$28.**

(5) Brooch, lacy sterling silver with rhinestones, **$65.**

(6) Beads, pressed glass, **$55.**

(7) Lavaliere, base metal. Chain and drop with characteristics of silver. The drop has blue paste stone, white enamel, **$75.**

(8) Brooch, pressed celluloid, coral in color, **$45.**

(9) Earrings, silver effect base metal; clear and pink imitation drops are faceted, **$32.**

(10) Brooch, early aluminum pin with etched design in black, marked "Coro." A find because very little aluminum jewelry is in circulation, **$45.**

(11) Earrings, mirror effect, set in charactertistics of silver with a base metal frame and screw posts, Art Deco, **$35.**

(12) Earrings, paste stones, sterling silver posts, **$32.**

(1) Heavyweight sterling silver acorn-leaf bracelet. Some of these bracelets are made in base metal, and one was reproduced recently in very thin sterling silver, **$65.**

(2) Necklace, sterling silver chain and imitation pearls, 13″ long. Has been reproduced, **$75.**

(3) Necklace, white enamel, center piece with a framed, milk glass drop, **$48.**

(4) Glass beads, ovals are flat black satin, very attractive, **$65.**

(5) Flower wreath brooch, with bow at bottom, sterling silver, **$45.**

(6) Charm, sailing ship, enameled on silver base metal, for a man's watchfob, **$50.**

(7) Large brooch, paste stones, silver-washed high relief, **$25.**

(8) Watch pin, Art Nouveau, iris and woman's head with flowing hair, sterling silver top, **$80.**

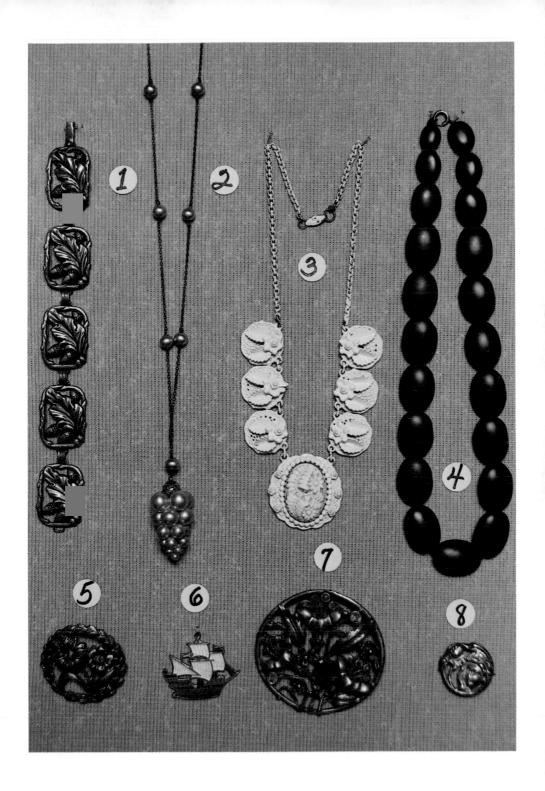

(1) Pendant, sterling silver, has cloisonné geese, **$38.**

(2) Locket, Art Deco, enamel with gold wash over brass, **$35.**

(3) Ring, adjustable, ornately made in copper with paste stones. Sides have pierced design, **$45.**

(4) Beads, white celluloid, screw type clasp, **$48.**

(5) Beads, red celluloid, 29″ long, **$65.**

(6) Beads, dyed horn. Some beads have both a pressed and pierced design, **$60.**

(7) Brooch, sterling silver, wild rose, **$65.**

(8) Brooch, amber paste stone in ornate gold wash over brass frame, **$35.**

(9) Buckle, dyed pearl set in characteristics of silver base metal frame, **$45.**

(10) Bracelet, copper mesh with gold washed ends. Imitation turquoise stones, safety chain. The two ends snap together, **$45.**

(11) Cameo, celluloid in oxidized base metal frame. Back has a hook for a chain, **$55.**

(1) Mosaic brooch, made in Italy, **$45.**

(2) Brooch, gold wash over brass, imitation pearl, **$28.**

(3) Brooch, gold plated, with design on textured background, **$28.**

(4) Pin, gold plate, **$32.**

(5) Lavaliere with paste blossoms, on chain with characteristics of silver, **$55.**

(6) Lavaliere, gold wash over copper, imitation onyx and pearl drop, **$65.**

(7) Beads, art glass. Inside the beads are tiny pink crystals. Celluloid screw fastener, **$65.**

(8) Pin, oxidized base metal with a thin silver wash. The pilgrims are John Alden and Priscilla Mullen, **$45.**

(9) Watch pin, sterling silver, **$65.**

(10) Brooch, gold wash over copper, imitation stones, **$28.**

(11) Brooch, cloisonné on sterling silver, **$55.**

(12) Bracelet, gold wash over brass, paste cabochon with transfers of figures, **$45.**

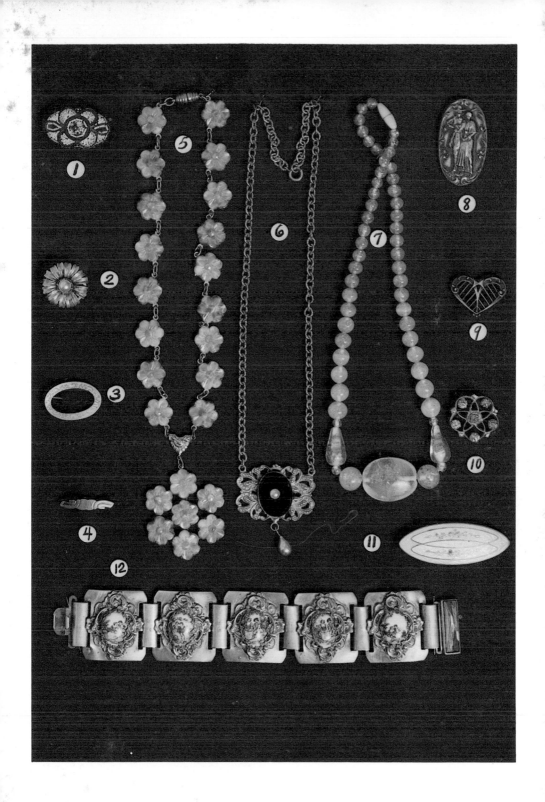

(1) Lavaliere, gold-washed, paste stones, delicate flat chain, **$95.**

(2) Bracelet of American Indian design, paste stones; band charateristic of silver, **$50.**

(3) Necklace, paste stones, probably Mexican Indian, **$90.**

(4) Bracelet, turquoise set in heavy sterling silver, **$95.**

(5) Brooch, sterling silver, paste stone, **$45.**

(6) Tiny buckle pin, enamel on copper, **$45.**

(7) Earrings, green turquoise inlaid in sterling silver, **$65.**

(8) Oval earrings, turquoise set in sterling silver, **$75.**

(9) Earrings, sterling silver frame, paste stones, **$40.**

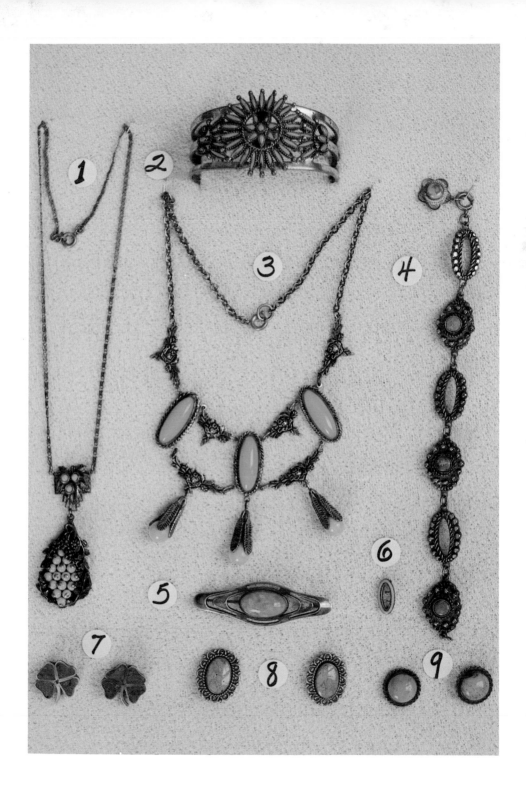

(1) Cuff links, elk's head of oxidized base metal, **$32.**

(2) Bracelet, sterling silver, **$75.**

(3) Beads, long, paste, hand-knotted, **$45.**

(4) Beads, glass with brass findings, **$65.**

(5) Beads, glass with lacy brass findings, **$45.**

(6) Cuff links, gold plated, dolphin in relief, **$55.**

(7) Ring, black onyx paste stone, gold-washed base metal, **$25.**

(8) Brooch, cloisonné, four Dutch girls, **$65.**

(9) Pin, flag in shape of a bow, marked "H" in triangle. Enamel on sterling, rare, **$55.**

(10) Bicentennial bracelet with Statue of Liberty, Liberty Bell, Paul Revere's Midnight Ride, Drummer Boy, and Minuteman. Base metal with characteristics of silver, **$75.**

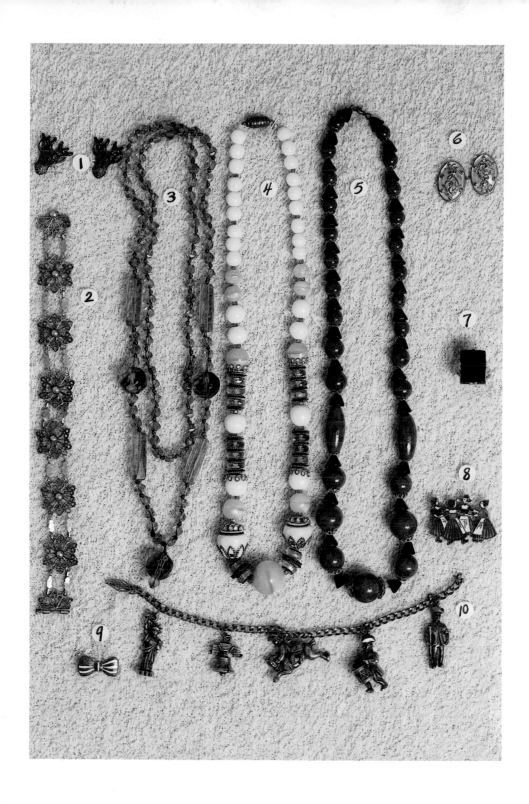

(1) Cross, sterling silver filigree, imitation pearls, **$95.**

(2) Earrings, imitation jet drops with screw posts in base metal, **$55.**

(3) Brooch, sterling silver filigree, **$75.**

(4) Cameo, pressed milk glass, religious figure in relief set in filigree, gold wash brass frame, **$65.**

(5) Lavaliere, pressed cameo bust applied to celluloid, **$55.**

(6) Bracelet, glass, pale amber beads, link chain, **$48.**

(7) Necklace, sterling silver, **$75.**

(8) Bracelet, flexible sterling silver, imitation stones, **$65.**

(9) Cuff links, sterling silver, pond lilies in relief, **$65.**

(10) Cuff links, enamel on sterling silver, **$55.**

(11) Brooch, brown imitation sard, with marcasites set in a base metal gilt frame, **$55.**

(12) Bracelet, sterling silver, all charms with moving parts except heart and horn, **$100.** *(Numbers 1 through 6 are from the collection of a friend.)*

(1) Earrings, sterling silver, **$45.**

(2) Earrings, topaz paste stones, gold-washed filigreed frames, **$28.**

(3) Bow earrings, gold-washed over sterling silver, **$55.**

(4) Earrings, amethyst paste stones, sterling silver, **$60.**

(5) Earrings, paste stones, gold-washed filigree, **$65.**

(6) Earrings, paste aquamarine stones, gold-washed frames, **$45.**

(7) Matching clip to No. 6, **$40.**

(8) Necklace, Art Deco, paste stone, **$85.**

(9) Brooch, mother-of-pearl, base metal frame. Small paste stone in pansy center, **$45.**

(10) Earrings, paste opals with three small rose pink stones, beautifully enameled, marked "Czechoslovakia," **$38.**

(11) Long earrings, gold-washed, paste stones, enameled, **$45.**

(12) Cameo earrings, oval celluloid cameo on glass set in a gold-washed frame, **$28.**

(13) Earrings, real coral set in sterling silver, **$65.**

(14) Belt and buckle earrings, gold-washed over brass, **$35.**

(15) Earrings, sterling silver bows, paste amethyst stones, **$65.**

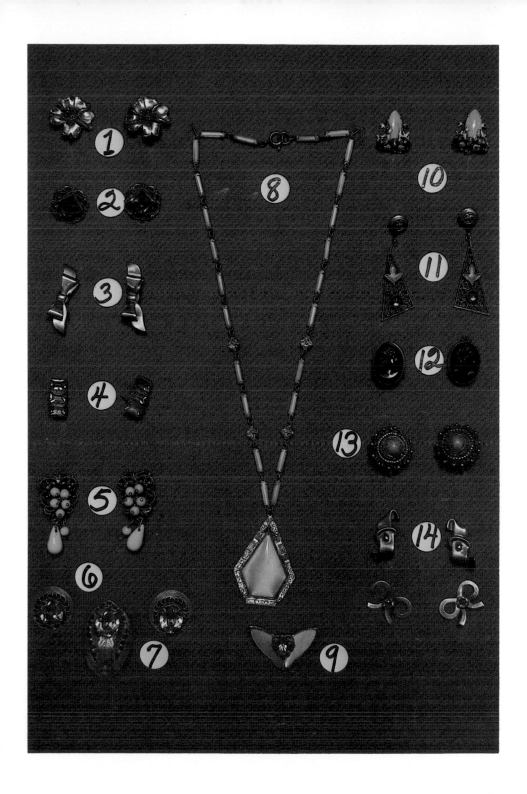

(1) Necklace, paste stones, unusual design, **$45.**

(2) Necklace, oxidized brass, paste stones in filigreed frame, **$65.**

(3) Brooch, ship enameled on a silver base metal, **$55.**

(4) Loop-over necklace, imitation pearls, sterling silver chain, **$65.**

(5) Loop-over necklace, unusual chain with pressed glass drops, **$85.**

(6) Brooch, buckle-shaped, Art Nouveau, characteristics of silver, **$55.**

(7) Brooch, gold-washed, pressed black stones, **$45.**

(8) Brooch, abalone set in sterling silver, **$58.**

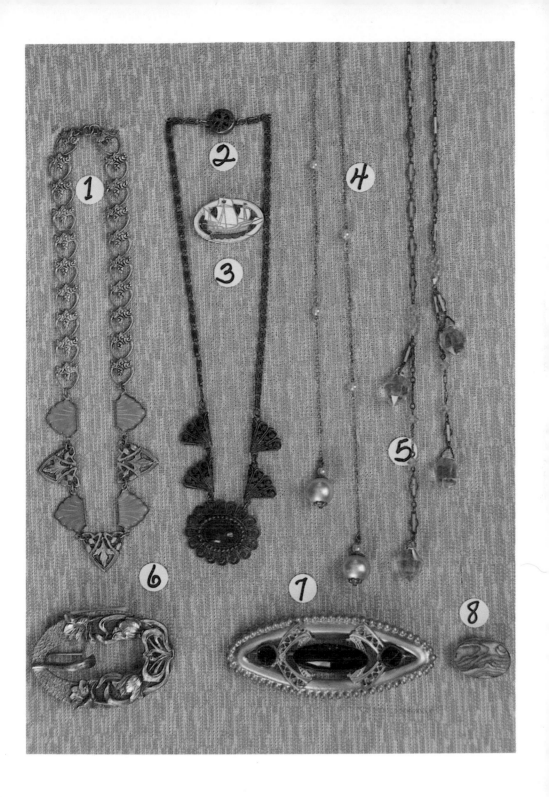

(1) Wooden beads, 27″ long, brass spacers, **$45.**

(2) Necklace, celluloid two-piece, black-and-white acorns, **$65.**

(3) Beads, imitation lapis lazuli, crystal beads, small brass spacers, chain, **$55.**

(4) Beads, cut crystal on chain, black glass spacers, **$65.**

(5) Earrings, screw posts, early plastic, **$30.**

(6) Earrings, American Indian style arrows with imitation turquoise, base metal, **$28.**

(7) Earrings, Art Deco, paste set in sterling silver, **$65.**

(8) Brooch, horse's heads, sterling silver, **$35.**

(9) Brooch, aluminum with imitation stones, **$48.**

(10) Bar pin, sterling silver with black enamel, rhinestones, **$65.**

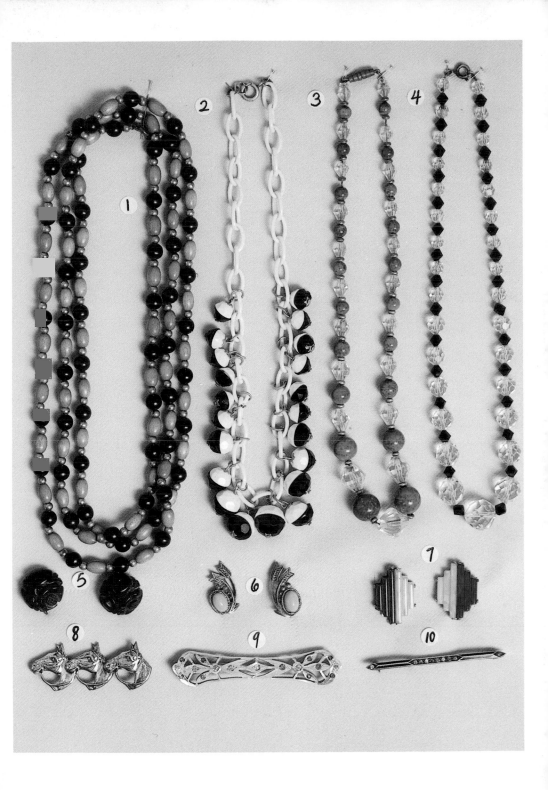

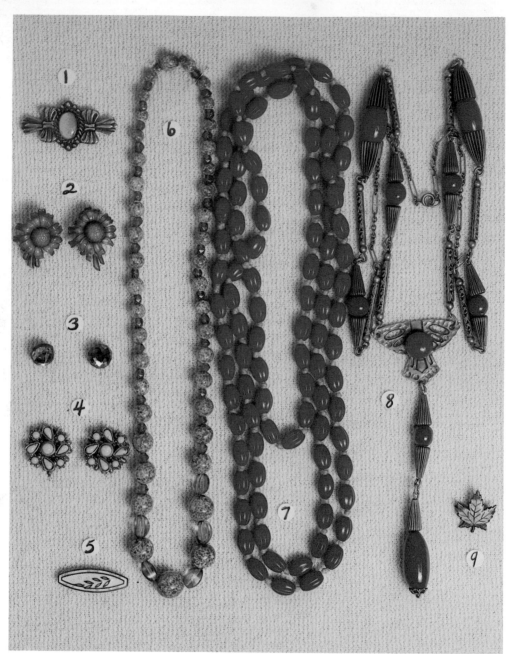

(1) Brooch, sterling silver, imitation turquoise, **$45.** (2) Earrings, slip-on type, all celluloid, **$38.** (3) Earrings, paste amethyst applied to base metal, screw posts, **$22.** (4) Earrings, paste turquoise applied to base metal, screw posts, **$22.** (5) Brooch, cloisonné, **$38.** (6) Beads, imitation lapis lazuli and amber. The fastener is a bead, **$75.** (7) Beads, melon-shaped, coral in color, knotted string, **$75.** (8) Necklace, brass chain and ornaments, paste beads, **$75.** (9) Leaf pin, enamel on base metal, **$28.**

Index

About the Author

S. Sylvia Henzel was educated in an industrial town in the Mohawk Valley in Upstate New York. After her marriage to Walter Henzel, the couple moved to Watervliet, New York. Mrs. Henzel has two sons.

At this time, a friend who collected buttons introduced Mrs. Henzel to that fascinating hobby. She began collecting and reading everything she could find on the subject. The collecting of old costume jewelry seemed to follow naturally. Her own sizable collection, carefully studied and researched, grew as her knowledge of the field expanded. This book, her third, follows the publication of *Old Costume Jewelry: A Collector's Dream with Prices* and *Collectible Costume Jewelry with Prices*. All were published by Wallace-Homestead Book Company.